Just As A Tree Grows

Short Poems That Stem From Within

Scherezad Yusef

BookLeaf Publishing

India | USA | UK

Made with ♥ on the BookLeaf Publishing Platform

www.bookleafpub.in

www.bookleafpub.com

To my mom, for always encouraging my creative side

To my brother, for being my biggest cheerleader

To my pup, for loving me no matter what

Preface

Just As A Tree Grows was the first poem I ever wrote as a child. I must have been around 7 years old. I scribbled it down in just a few minutes and drew a tree on the other side of the page, just a simple piece of notebook paper. It was a simile, comparing the growth of a tree to the growth of our family and friends and our home.

My parents were surprisingly impressed with it, which was a rarity. They loved it so much that they stuck it up in our house, taped to a cabinet in the kitchen, where everyone could see it. Through everything our family endured, my parents didn't take it down until we moved out. How I wish I had kept that poem safe.

Writing that poem was the first time I ever felt like a writer. I buried that feeling deeply for years afterward, but a part of me always knew that I would return to it. In this book, I rewrote that poem, from a different lens this time. I don't think it lives up to its original, but the bones are still there. This is my first poetry book. I hope you enjoy reading it as much as I enjoyed writing it.

Why Am I Here?

I did not come here to take up space,
To fall in love with myself or to be deserving
of something more
I did not come here to prove my worth,
To be a goddess, or a queen, or a star
I came here quietly, with a book in my hand,
To have a laugh, and to love too much
Sometimes I get distracted, and I'm louder
than I want to be,
Maybe I'm trying to fit in, with people more
normal than me
But deep down inside, I'm just a girl with a
book,
Who just wants to sit on a tree branch and
read
Some sunshine and a life of peace and
simplicity,
Is really all I need

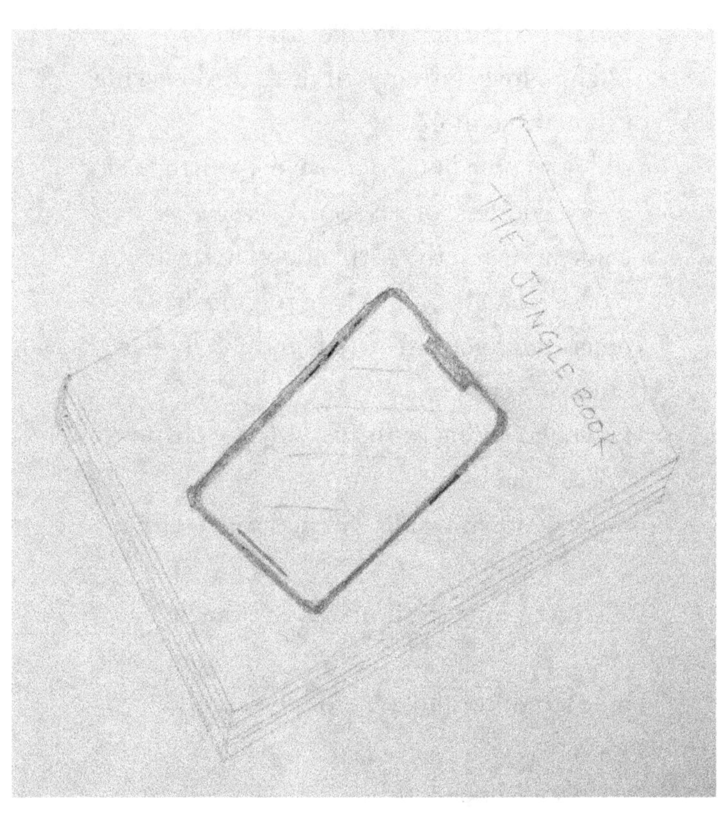

THE JUNGLE BOOK

Lessons

When I was young, I was taught that
If you say one thing,
Then do another,
Your character comes into question
But when I grew up, I learned that
Few truly assess one another's character—
Not really, anyway
They don't know how
Or maybe they don't know that they should
So, as a result,
Many say one thing,
Then do another,
And no one asks any questions
At all

The Chase

I've always chased after what I wanted,
Even when what I wanted didn't want me
Now, I want for nothing at all,
But without the need to chase,
I don't know who I am—
Only who I was
I have nowhere to run,
No direction to move in
It's like time is standing still,
But I know it isn't,
Only I am

The Leak

5

Moving on is like having a leak in your brain.
It doesn't happen all at once—
It's a slow, gradual movement
Day by day,
Bit by bit,
Until, eventually, the memories are all
drained away,
Taking up less space in your brain
Less energy to revisit
And then, finally,
One day,
There's no pain associated with them anymore
The memories appear and then disappear
Like clouds floating by
One minute, they're there,
The next minute, they're gone
And suddenly you're at peace,
Without even realizing it

Sacrifice

You always have to give something away if you
want to have something
This life will make you feel very far away from
home
Like you have to sacrifice everything you
know
The comforts you once had
Must be removed if you want to grow
The pain you once ran from
Must become your new addiction
You cannot escape it
There are no shortcuts, though you'll try to
find them
But it's only once you stop searching that
you'll see
You always have to give something away if you
want to have something

Sometimes I

Sometimes I wish I were younger
Sometimes I wish I were smarter
Sometimes I wish I were stronger
More flexible
More talented
More beautiful
More
But then I realize—
I am who I am
I am who I'm supposed to be
I am where I'm meant to be
Instead of wishing
Maybe I could just appreciate being me

Dirty Slut

The meaning of words change
Depending on who says them,
Who hears them,
The tone they were spoken in,
Or how they were written
Depending on who wrote them,
The time they were said,
The emotions of the one who received them

The meaning of words can be so deep
Or shallow
Words can be life altering
Or they can mean nothing at all
You get to choose their impact—
Or do you?

What If

What if none of this is real
And it's all a simulation?
What if we're stuck in the matrix
And we don't even know it?
What if we can't unplug
And we have to survive the computer
program?
What if we don't have a choice
And we can't escape it?

What do we do then?
Does this life mean anything at all?
If we're all just batteries powering the robots
That we designed and built ourselves?
We created our own demons
And when they came to haunt us
We were surprised

As if it wasn't our own doing
That led to our demise

The Clock

There's no time like the present,
Because in the present, there's no time
No future, and no past,
In the present, time doesn't move
It doesn't have to
There's only the moment you're in,
And your full commitment to it
There's no need to look outside,
Only within
And within us, there is no concept of time
Time is a social construct we live by,
Regretting the past,
Plotting for the future,
But only if we're not living in the present

Second Life

I never understood the allure of a second life
Until I met social media
I thought it was the most obviously and
pathetically escapist concept—
A virtual second life?
When you have a physical one already?
For what?
But now I understand
That sometimes, this life is not easy—
Many times, in fact
And living in that second life,
Where only perfect moments are shown,
Where you are only your best self—
And nothing and no one else—
It's the only thing keeping you from giving up
altogether
It's both a prison and a haven
It prevents you from making your physical
life better,
But it keeps you from having to accept your
treacherous reality—
Which perhaps you don't have the strength to
do

A toxic cycle
So you keep filming your highlight reel,
In hopes that the darkness of your reality will
one day fade
But deep down, you know the truth—
That if you don't face the darkness,
You'll never be able to live a better life offline
Even still, some days you're not even sure you
want to

The Journey

It's been a painful journey away from myself,
And a painful journey coming back to myself
With painful lessons along the way
I've learned a lot, but I am tired
And many times I still lose sight of who I am
They say sometimes you have to leave yourself
to find yourself
I left myself, then found myself,
Then disappeared entirely
You see, being somebody isn't all it's cracked
up to be
It's being nobody that's the key
Being somebody is like wearing a costume—
But once you take it off,
That's when you're really free

Flowers

Everything is connected
Plants, animals, people, the earth, and the sea
This is where we are meant to be,
This is how we ascend
This place of oneness is a place of higher
vibrations
We are meant to open up like flowers,
We grow from seeds and slowly bloom
Our petals reach towards the sun—
The final state is this
The understanding of the connection,
An appreciation for everything that we are—
Collectively, non-dually
Youth is believing this is crazy
Maturation is realizing this is the truth
We are the flowers
We are one

The Museum

My mind is like a museum now—
It's wide open and bright, with lots of space
for new exhibits
But there are some old ones too
Sometimes, I stop by the artifacts I don't even
enjoy anymore,
Because they make me feel something
Because when I'm tired, it's easy and familiar
But then, I catch myself in a moment,
And I move on—either to empty space,
Or to something simpler, something I can
appreciate
I want to keep filling this museum with new
and beautiful pieces,
So that the old ones I dislike are fewer and far
between
I can't just get rid of them, they are part of
my history
They are still art,
Invoking sadness, anxiety, fear, disgust
I can get further away from them,
They can be less significant, less visceral,
But I know this will take time

So I am settling in the difficult discomfort
Years from now, this museum will be
completely different
A year ago, it was completely different
And for that, I am grateful

Reality Is A Memory

Reality is subjective
It comes from a memory of a moment in time
Yet, we define "reality" as objective
The state of things as they actually exist
Rather than as they may appear or are
imagined to be
But the state of things as they actually exist
Depends on how one perceives their
appearance
What you see and what I see will never be the
same
Even if we are looking at the same thing at
the same time
Nothing can be real
Nothing can be true
Everything is a figment of our imagination
There is no such thing as a fact anymore
I don't know if there ever was

Too Much

I love too much
I laugh too much
I worry too much
I cry too much
I fall too much
I read too much
I think too much
I run too much
I hide too much
I play too much
I try too much
I yell too much
I live too much
But somehow, I still believe I'm not enough

The Never-Ending Playground

The internet is a playground
We look around and see other children—
Climbing,
Sliding,
Running,
Jumping,
Hanging,
Swinging,
Throwing,
Playing
We want to be like them
We don't want to be like them
We fall down
We get back up
We want to learn
We don't want to learn
We just want to play
We have to go to the playground, day and
night
We cannot leave
We won't grow up

We won't move on
We don't want to play anymore
But it's too late—
We can't stop going to the playground

Mermaid

I'm stranded on land,
Like a fish out of water
I was never meant to live this way
I can breathe, but barely—
This is no way of life for a mermaid
I am forced to survive in a world where
people have legs
Their feet touch the ground
They walk with purpose and productivity,
Driven by fear and rage
My fins thrash against it all,
Desperately flipping and flopping—
I want to go back to the sea
There, I am beautiful and smart and capable
I flow with the ocean, graceful and free
In this world I'm trapped, suffocated,
incompetent
If only they could see me
Where I'm supposed to be

Lessons Part 2

My mother always told me,
What goes around comes around
If you are kind,
You will receive kindness
If you are selfish,
The world will be cruel
If you steal,
You will be punished
You may not immediately realize
The consequences of your actions
But as time passes
You will become wise
And you will see—
That for every action you take,
There is an equal and opposite reaction
So try to be good,
And good will always come to you

Our Grandfather's Laugh

Hearty laughs that travel from generation to
generation,
Down the bloodline, full and substantial
Contagious, clever, and silly all at once,
We all got their humor, not one of us missed
out
We laugh and tell one another jokes and
stories freely
Soaking them all in, so full of love
So that even long after our grandfathers are
gone,
Their laughter echoes through each one of us
Living inside us,
Until they are passed down to the little ones
that come next

Hypocrisy

This is both
Too soon yet overdue
Overused yet brand new
Exclusive yet uncool
You brought out the hypocrite
But it's genuine

Woke a demon up from her slumber
Summoned an angel down from the heavens
Let the lioness out the jungle—
Untamed, yet destined for fame
Notoriety
Hiding in plain sight
Privacy was a privilege
I always had to learn the simplest lessons the
hard way,
But this one was child's play

No biting
Not biting my tongue, no more
How many times did you use the word *whore*?
Stupid, worthless, bitch, and more?
But *abuse* is too big a word, even for you

You revel in it,
Bask in it,
Soak in its glow,
Just so you can feel something
No—
Abuse gives you power you never had within
You didn't earn it
I'm not a victim
The power you felt was the power I generated
that only flowed through you,
Like an electrical current

You're a monster of my own creation
Frankenstein
I'm the villain in this story—
Dr. Jekyll and Mr. Hyde
You were nothing but a vessel for a lesson that
God was trying to teach me long before you
arrived
He sent you to me because I wouldn't
comply,
I wouldn't listen because I wasn't alive
I wasn't awake yet

Both here and in a past life, I've sinned
But it had to stop, it had to end,
It had to be finished
It's finally over, done with—
Killed, dead, murdered, buried
The phoenix rises from ashes and dirt—
Rebirth

Just As A Tree Grows

Just as a tree grows,
Its roots into the ground,
Its trunk up to the sky,
Its branches out wide,
We grow too
We ground ourselves,
We reach for the stars,
We become old and wise

Just as a tree grows,
Taking its time,
Living off of the necessary nutrients
The sun and sky and water and soil
Slowly but surely,
We grow too
Growth comes with time, effort, and
sustenance
It doesn't happen overnight
We survive off of what is in our vicinity,
What we choose to keep around,
Until one day, we find ourselves
Like a huge, old tree,
Grown from the nature that surrounds us

Just as a tree grows,
It sits rooted through rain or shine,
Through darkness and light,
Through beauty and pain,
Shedding its leaves as the seasons change—
We grow too
Life changes, moving quickly around us
But our true self remains within
Sometimes we get further away from who we
really are,
Through challenges and successes,
Through courage and fear
We always come back to ourselves,
Like a tree always comes back to its roots

Just as a tree grows,
So do we
It's a beautiful thing to see